MY FIRST
BIBLE

MY FIRST BIBLE
Learning About God's Special People
First published by Scandinavia Publishing House
Copyright © 2004
This edition published by The Stanborough Press Ltd,
Alma Park, Grantham, NG31 9SL, England.
Copyright © 2006
Text by Leyah Jensen
Illustrations by Gustavo Mazali
Design by Ben Alex
ISBN 1-904685-22-6
Printed in China

MY FIRST BIBLE

LEARNING ABOUT GOD'S SPECIAL PEOPLE

Text by Leyah Jensen

Illustrations by
Gustavo Mazali

SP

The Stanborough Press Ltd.

Contents

In the beginning

In the beginning, there was only darkness—and God. But God said, "Let there be light!" The light became day and the darkness became night. Then God separated heaven from water, and water from earth. He filled the sky with birds, the water with fish, and the land with animals. Then he made a man named Adam and a woman named Eve to care for the earth. At last God rested, very pleased with all He had created.

Genesis 1:1–31

Noah builds a boat

The people in the world stopped listening to God and became wicked, so God decided to start over with a good man named Noah. He told Noah to build a big boat and fill it with every kind of animal. When it began to rain, Noah and his family went inside the boat. Then it rained until the whole earth was flooded. Finally, the water dried and they could come onto the land again. God put a rainbow in the sky as a reminder of His promise to never drown the earth again.
Genesis 6:1–8:22

9

Isaac is born

God was happy with Abraham and Sarah. He promised they would become parents of a great nation. But when they were very old, they still had no children.

One day three angels came by and said they would soon have a son. Sarah laughed—how could an old woman have a baby?

Yet God was faithful to Abraham and Sarah. They had a son, Isaac. A great nation came from Isaac, as God had promised.

Genesis 21:1-7

Joseph's dream

Isaac had a son named Jacob, and Jacob had many sons of his own. Joseph was Jacob's favorite son, and this made the others angry. One night, Joseph dreamed he would someday rule his brothers. When he told his brothers the dream, they became even more angry.

One day they saw him coming and said, "Let's kill him
and tell our father it was a wild animal!" One of the
brothers convinced them to sell him instead. Their
father believed Joseph had been killed, and he was
very sad.
Genesis 37:1–36

Joseph in Egypt

Joseph was taken to Egypt to be a slave, yet God was with him. His masters saw that Joseph was very wise and trusted him.

One day Pharaoh, the King of Egypt, had a frightening dream. None of his wise men could tell him what it meant. But then Pharaoh learned about Joseph. Joseph told Pharaoh what God was telling him in the dream. Pharaoh was so thankful that he set Joseph free, and made him his chief minister! Then Joseph brought his family to Egypt. He forgave his brothers, and they all lived happily together.

Genesis 39:1–47:31

14

Moses, prince of Egypt

Many years later, a new Pharaoh was not so kind to Joseph's family, the Israelites. He turned all the Israelites into slaves.

An Israelite woman had a baby. She wanted to save her son from the cruel Pharaoh, so she sent him down the river in a basket. Just then, Pharaoh's daughter was taking a bath in the river. She found the baby and named him Moses. Then she took him home, and Moses grew up in Pharaoh's palace.

Exodus 2:1–10

Moses leads the people out of Egypt

Moses realized that Pharaoh was treating his people unfairly, so he ran away from Egypt. Yet God sent Moses back to tell Pharaoh that he should let the Israelites go. Moses performed miracles to prove his message was from God. At last the Israelites were freed, and they hurried towards the desert. Soon Pharaoh changed his mind, and chased them with his army. But God parted the sea so that the Israelites could escape to safety. Then they praised God!

Exodus 13:17–14:31

19

God's people in the desert

The Israelites stayed in the desert forty years, and God provided for them. Through Moses, God passed His laws on to the people.

   When Moses died, Joshua became the leader. God told Joshua to be strong and courageous. Then Joshua brought the Israelites out of the desert and into the land of milk and honey that God had promised them.

Joshua 1:1–18

The walls of Jericho

The Israelites came to a great city called Jericho.
Though it was surrounded by a wall of stone, God said
He would help them win the city. Joshua led the people
as God had instructed, marching around the city with
trumpets for six days. On the seventh day, they
marched around the city seven times. Then the priests
blew the horns, and all the Israelites shouted. Suddenly,
the walls of Jericho crumbled before their eyes!

Joshua 5:13–6:27

God makes Samson strong

The Israelites settled in the new land, Israel. There they had new enemies called the Philistines. Yet God was going to help them once again. He sent a man named Samson, so strong that he could kill a lion with his bare hands! Samson took revenge on the Philistines. When they tried to capture him, God gave him the power to beat an entire army alone. Samson helped protect the Israelites for twenty years.
Judges 13:1–16:31

God helps Ruth

One day there was not enough food in Israel, so a man and his wife Naomi went to Moab. Their sons got married there. But then the man and his sons died. Naomi told her daughters-in-law to go home to their parents. Ruth would not listen; she wanted to go back to Israel with Naomi. Ruth took care of Naomi in Israel, and God blessed them. He gave Ruth a new husband, as well.
Ruth 1:1–4:22

David the shepherd boy

David was the great-grandson of Ruth. He was the smallest of his brothers, so while his brothers fought the Philistines, David tended his father's sheep.

But God saw that David's heart was good. He chose David to be the king of Israel someday.

1 Samuel 16:1–13

David kills Goliath

The Israelites were afraid of the Philistines because they had a giant, named Goliath. Goliath dared the Israelites to find a man strong enough to fight him.

Finally, there was a volunteer—it was the shepherd boy, David! The king gave David armor, but it was too big. So David walked up to the giant with only a slingshot. The giant was ready to squash him, but then David flung a stone into the giant's forehead. David had killed the giant! The Philistines were defeated, and David later became king of Israel.

1 Samuel 17:1-58

Solomon the Wise

David's son Solomon became the next king. God loved Solomon. When Solomon prayed, he didn't ask for riches, but for wisdom so that he could be a good king. This made God so happy that He gave Solomon both wisdom and riches.

32

God promised Solomon that he would be the wisest man that would ever live. People came from near and far to ask his advice.
1 Kings 3:16–28

33

God sends fire

Many years later, there was a bad king who didn't listen to God. Some of the Israelites had even begun to worship a false god named Baal. But then God sent Elijah to show the king and the Israelites who the true God was. Elijah took the people to a hilltop, and told them to ask Baal to light a fire. They prayed and prayed, but no fire came. Then Elijah prayed to God. Suddenly, an enormous fire lighted. Now everyone knew who the true God was!

1 Kings 18:16–46

Queen Esther

Esther was an Israelite living in Persia. One day, the king of Persia decided to make Esther his queen. One of the king's men became angry that the Israelites would only worship God. He asked to have the Israelites in Persia killed, and the king agreed. The Israelites were very worried. But then Queen Esther went to the king and told him her secret—that she was an Israelite herself! The king agreed to save her people. Esther's courage had rescued the Israelites.

Esther 1:1-10:3

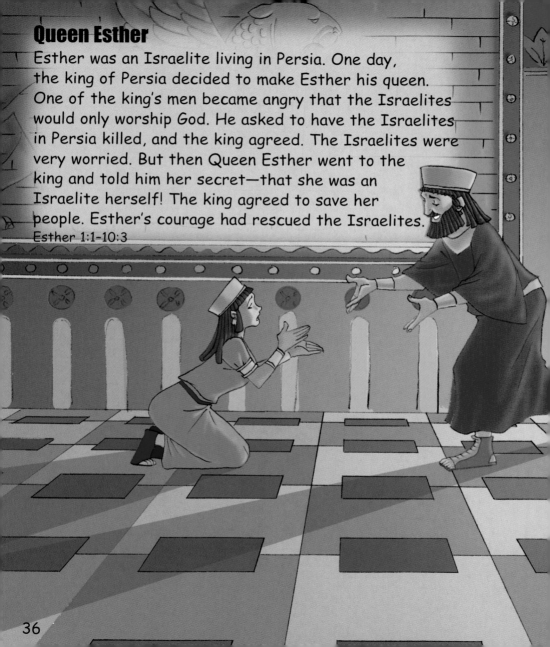

God saves Daniel and his friends

The king of Babylon built a statue of gold, and ordered everyone in the kingdom to worship it. But three Israelites named
Shadrach, Meshach and Abednego refused to worship any-
thing but God. The king was so angry that he threw them into
a fiery furnace. But then the king looked into the flames and
saw four figures standing, unharmed! God had sent an angel to
protect the three men. The king then knew that theirs was
the true God, and worshiped with them. Daniel 3:1–30

Daniel and the lions

The king of Babylon could see that God was with Daniel, so he gave Daniel care of his kingdom. The other leaders were jealous, so they planned a trick. They got the king to order everyone to worship him for thirty days. When Daniel did not obey, he was thrown into the lions' den. But God shut the mouths' of the lions. The next morning, the king looked into the den. He was happy to see Daniel alive, and ordered everyone to worship only God.

Daniel 6:1–28

Jonah and the fish

God told Jonah to go to a city
called Nineveh and tell them
God was angry with them.
Jonah didn't want to go, so he
tried to run away on a ship.

But God sent a huge storm, and Jonah was tossed overboard. Then a giant fish swallowed him. Inside the fish, Jonah prayed. So God had the fish spit Jonah onto dry land. Then Jonah went to Nineveh and gave them God's message, and they stopped being wicked.
Jonah 1:1–4:11

Jesus is born

An angel came to a woman named Mary and said, "You will give birth to the Son of God!" Then Jesus was born in a stable in Bethlehem. When the shepherds heard the news, they came to see the baby. Three wise men saw a star in the sky and brought baby Jesus gifts. Luke 2:1-20

Jesus heals people

Jesus taught people how to follow God. He
traveled from town to town, telling people to
love God and love each other. Jesus laid his
hands on the sick, and healed them. He took
the children on his knees and blessed them,
though others wanted to send them away.
People came from all around to listen to Jesus
and see him perform miracles.
Mark:5:35–43

Jesus feeds people

One day, Jesus was teaching on a hilltop. The people began to get hungry, but there was no food for them to eat. Then one of the disciples found a boy with just five loaves of bread and two small fish. Jesus began to break the food. Before their eyes, Jesus turned the small meal into enough to feed all five thousand people!
Matthew 14:13–21

Jesus the good shepherd

Jesus told stories to help people understand his teachings.
In one story, he described how the good shepherd would give
his life to protect his sheep. He knew each one of his sheep,
and if he lost one he would search until he found it. Jesus said
that he was like the good shepherd towards the people that
followed him.
Luke 15:1–7

Jesus stills the storm

One evening, Jesus and the disciples were crossing a lake in their boat. Jesus was sleeping. Suddenly it became dark, and a storm grew. The disciples were afraid. "Jesus, save us! We are going to drown!" they cried. Jesus got up and told the wind and the waves to quiet down. The disciples were amazed and said, "Look, even the wind and the waves obey Jesus!"
Matt. 8:23-27

Jesus visits Zacchaeus

Zacchaeus was a tiny man that nobody liked much because he cheated people. But when Jesus came to town, Zacchaeus wanted to see him too.

Zacchaeus was too short to see over the people, so he climbed into a tree. When Jesus passed the tree, he looked up at Zacchaeus and asked to visit him.

Though others thought Zacchaeus was bad, Jesus wanted to be his friend. Zacchaeus was so happy that he promised to give back to people what he had taken from them.   Luke 19:1-10

55

King Jesus

More and more people believed that Jesus was truly the Son of God. One day he rode to Jerusalem on a donkey, and a huge crowd greeted him along the road. They waved palm branches and sang songs, praising him for the miracles they had seen. The people wanted Jesus to be their king. But Jesus hadn't come to rule them; he had come to die for their sins.

Matthew 21:1–11

58

The last meal

Jesus knew it was almost time for him to return to his Father in heaven, so he gathered his disciples around him for the last supper. He asked them to remember him when they ate from now on. He told them not to be sad when he had gone, because someday he would return to bring them to heaven too. In the meantime, they should love one another and teach others to do the same.
Luke 22:7–23

Jesus is killed

The next day, the leaders of Israel came to arrest Jesus. They didn't believe that he was the Son of God. They decided to kill Jesus, and all of his friends were very sad. But Jesus knew it was God's will.

The soldiers took him to a hilltop and hung him on the cross. Jesus asked God to forgive those who had hurt him. Then Jesus died.

Mark 15:1–47

Jesus lives

Easter morning, Jesus' friend Mary went to his tomb. But two angels sat where his body had been. Then she saw Jesus standing up, alive and well!

That evening, Jesus came to his disciples. They saw that he had risen from the dead as he had promised, and were overjoyed. Jesus told them to spread his teachings throughout the world. Then Jesus left them and returned to Heaven.

But he sent the Holy Spirit to help them spread the word about him.

Mark 16:1–20

Happiness in Heaven

The disciple John dreamed that he saw Jesus in Heaven, surrounded by all his friends. Then John knew they would see Jesus again. In heaven there would be no more pain or sadness, only happiness and joy.
Revelation 21:1–8

God's special people

The stories in the Bible show how much God loves people. God loves every person so much that everyone is special to Him. He loves us so very much that He sent His own son to die for us so we can be with Him in Heaven after we die.